FOOD WEBS

I0794068

MOUNTAIN

Food Webs

By William Anthony

KidHaven PUBLISHING

Published in 2021 by
KidHaven Publishing, an Imprint of Greenhaven Publishing, LLC
353 3rd Avenue
Suite 255
New York, NY 10010

Edited by: Madeline Tyler
Designed by: Jasmine Pointer

Find us on

Cataloging-in-Publication Data

Names: Anthony, William.
Title: Mountain food webs / William Anthony.
Description: New York : KidHaven Publishing, 2021. | Series: Food webs | Includes glossary and index.
Identifiers: ISBN 9781534535244 (pbk.) | ISBN 9781534535268 (library bound) | ISBN 9781534535251 (6 pack) | ISBN 9781534535275 (ebook)
Subjects: LCSH: Mountain ecology--Juvenile literature. | Mountain animals--Juvenile literature. | Food chains (Ecology)--Juvenile literature.
Classification: LCC QH541.5.M65 A584 2021 | DDC 577.5'3--dc23

Printed in the United States of America

CPSIA compliance information: Batch #BS20K: For further information contact Greenhaven Publishing LLC, New York, New York at 1-844-317-7404.

Please visit our website, www.greenhavenpublishing.com. For a free color catalog of all our high-quality books, call toll free 1-844-317-7404 or fax 1-844-317-7405.

Photo credits:
Images are courtesy of Shutterstock.com with thanks to Getty Images, Thinkstock Photo, and iStockphoto.

YamabikaY (paper texture). Front cover - Abeselom Zerit, valzan, Eric Isselee, Thipwan, mcmortgreen. 2 - Pascal RATEAU. 3 - valzan. 4 & 5 - Daniel Prudek. 6 - 99Art, SeeVera, encikAn. 7 - Abydos, Chaithanya Krishnan, S. Shankar [CC BY 2.0 (https://creativecommons.org/licenses/by/2.0)], via Wikimedia Commons 6 & 7 - Big Foot Productions. 8 - Suman_Ghosh. 9 - Iakov Filimonov, Ashit choudhary, hejrazdvatri, DavidRebata. 10 - Vijay Kirve. 11 - Martin Mecnarowski, Ovchinnikova Irina, feathercollector, Milan Cherian. 12 - Vladimir Melnik. 13 - Kevin Standage, Alexey Seafarer, Ovchinnikova Irina, Alexandr Junek Imaging. 14 - RealityImages. 15 - Ana Gram, Victor Suarez Naranjo, KMW Photography. 16 - Dennis W Donohue. 17 - clarst5, saurabhsawant, scooperdigital. 18 - OSTILL is Franck Camhi. 19 - Anan Kaewkhammul, iaminut, Alexey Seafarer, Aivars Ivbulis. 20 - Thipwan, modus_vivendi. 21 - Thipwan, Edwin Butter, Tom Versteege, Petr Tkachev.

CONTENTS

Words that look like THIS can be found in the glossary on page 24.

IN THE MOUNTAINS

Go for a hike, see the beautiful sights... but be careful! Do you know who might be hiding behind the rocks, looking for a meal?

There are lots of different animals and plants to be found, all going about their daily business, and each and every one of them has a place in the food web.

Let's look at who eats who in the mountains. What can we find in the Asian Himalayas?

THE FOOD WEB

It all starts with the sun's energy...

...which feeds plants...

...**HERBIVORES** eat the plants...

...**CARNIVORES** eat the herbivores...

...bigger **PREDATORS** eat them...

...and **APEX PREDATORS** eat those.

THE HIMALAYAN WOLF

Careful—I'm a wolf, and I'm not alone. I'm one of the apex predators in these mountains. What puts me at the top of the food web is that I don't hunt for PREY alone. I always stick with my PACK. We work as a team to find our dinner.

NAME:	Himalayan Wolf
TYPE:	MAMMAL
HOME:	Asia
FOOD:	Carnivore
PREDATOR OR PREY?:	Apex Predator

I wonder what will be on our menu today...

Himalayan ibex: a large lunch...?

Bharal: a furry feast...?

Himalayan goral: a horned meal...?

It's the ibex for us today. We'll take our share and move on. I'm sure someone will be around for the scraps after we've gone!

WHO'S COMING THIS WAY?

THE GOLDEN JACKAL

Wherever those wolves go, we jackals are not far behind. Why would we put ourselves in danger when we can just eat the wolves' leftovers? Those ibex leftovers were tasty, but I'm still hungry...

NAME:	Golden Jackal
TYPE:	Mammal
HOME:	Asia and Europe
FOOD:	Carnivore
PREDATOR OR PREY?:	Both

I only need a snack,
but what should I have?

Woolly hare: jumpy but juicy...?

Insects: a tiny treat...?

Himalayan marmot: a delicious dinner...?

I think I want a bit of marmot for my dinner today. The only problem is finding it...

WHERE'S THE MARMOT?

THE HIMALAYAN MARMOT

Shhh! Keep quiet until that jackal has gone! We're marmots, and we all live together in a BURROW underground. We're OMNIVORES, which means that we eat both plants and other animals.

NAME:	Himalayan Marmot
TYPE:	Mammal
HOME:	Asia
FOOD:	Omnivore
PREDATOR OR PREY?:	Both

We have to compete with all of these animals. They eat shrubs and grass too.

Himalayan tahr: a big competitor...

Himalayan musk deer: a furry problem...

Woolly hare: a jumpy rival...

They're so annoying! In fact, there's a hare now. I'm sure one of its predators will scare it away soon...

QUICK, TURN THE PAGE!

THE WOOLLY HARE

I feel bad for taking those marmots' shrubs, but I need to eat when I can. I'm a woolly hare, and there are lots of predators looking for me. That's why I'm hiding behind this rock!

NAME:	Woolly Hare
TYPE:	Mammal
HOME:	Central Asia
FOOD:	Herbivore
PREDATOR OR PREY?:	Prey

These animals all want me as part of their dinner menu, so I try to stay out of sight.

Himalayan wolf: a big pack...

Golden jackal: sharp teeth...

Snow leopard: vicious claws...

Wait, what's that rustling in the leaves? I'm getting out of here!

OFF I GO!

THE SNOW LEOPARD

No! She got away! That hare was going to be my dinner, but now I'm going to have to find something else instead. Good thing I'm an apex predator! Finding food shouldn't be all that hard.

NAME:	Snow Leopard
TYPE:	Mammal
HOME:	Asia
FOOD:	Carnivore
PREDATOR OR PREY?:	Apex Predator

Himalayan tahr: a tasty treat...?

Red panda: a satisfying snack...?

Himalayan ibex: a yummy meal...?

No, none of these are quite good enough. Hang on... what's that? I hear big footsteps coming this way...

WHO IS IT?

THE ASIAN BLACK BEAR

What a long day! I'm an Asian black bear, and I'm an apex predator, just like the wolf and the snow leopard. I'm worn out from chasing my prey all day. I love having so many yummy choices!

NAME:	Asian Black Bear
TYPE:	Mammal
HOME:	Asia
FOOD:	Omnivore
PREDATOR OR PREY?:	Apex Predator

Himalayan marmot: full of flavor...

Himalayan musk deer: mouth-watering...

Berries: wonderfully juicy...

They all sound so great to me, but it's been such a long day. I think I need a nap instead.

WHO'S LEFT?

THE YELLOW-THROATED MARTEN

Although I'm not one of the top predators, I certainly act like one! I'm fearless, and not much will try to eat me—unless they want a good fight! I might be little, but I'm one fierce animal! I also smell bad, so predators like to stay away.

NAME:	Yellow-Throated Marten
TYPE:	Mammal
HOME:	Asia
FOOD:	Omnivore
PREDATOR OR PREY?:	Predator

I'm an omnivore, so I've got both plants and animals to choose from for my dinner!

Red panda: a colorful dish...

Himalayan musk deer: a tasty dinner...

Berries: a sweet snack...

I'm feeling very greedy tonight—I might even treat myself to a three-course meal and have all of them!

MOUNTAIN FOOD WEB

The arrows follow where the energy goes. Can you follow the energy from the sun all the way to the apex predators?

PRODUCER	Makes its own food using energy from the sun.
CONSUMER	Eats producers or other consumers.
APEX PREDATOR	Nothing eats it.

GLOSSARY

apex predator The top predator in a food chain, with no natural predators of its own.

burrow A hole or tunnel dug by an animal.

carnivore An animal that eats other animals instead of plants.

herbivore An animal that eats plants instead of other animals.

mammal An animal that has warm blood, a backbone, and produces milk.

omnivore An animal that eats both plants and other animals.

pack A group of the same animal (for example, wolves).

predator An animal that hunts other animals for food.

prey Animals that are hunted for food.

INDEX